INTRODUCTION

Are you seeking a culinary adventure that harmonizes the joys of food with the principles of diabetes management? Look no further! "Deliciously Diabetic" is a cookbook designed specifically for individuals living with diabetes or those looking to embrace a balanced and nutritious lifestyle.

With its delectable array of recipes, this cookbook combines the essence of culinary creativity with the wisdom of mindful eating. Each recipe has been thoughtfully crafted to ensure a balance of flavors, textures, and nutrients, while keeping in mind the dietary needs and restrictions of those managing diabetes.

Inside "Deliciously Diabetic," you will discover a wide range of dishes that cater to various tastes and occasions. From vibrant salads bursting with freshness to hearty mains and indulgent desserts, every recipe has been carefully crafted to offer a satisfying experience without compromising on flavor or health.

Whether you're newly diagnosed or have been managing diabetes for years, "Deliciously Diabetic" is your guide to embracing a delicious, fulfilling, and diabetic-friendly culinary lifestyle. It's time to savor the flavors and rediscover the joy of cooking, while keeping your health at the forefront.

Welcome to the world of "Deliciously Diabetic" where you can nourish your body, indulge your taste buds, and embrace the pleasures of food, one delightful recipe at a time. Let the journey to wellness and culinary delight begin!

Chicken & Spinach Skillet Pasta with Lemon & Parmesan

Ingredients:

8 ounces pasta (such as penne or fusilli)
2 boneless, skinless chicken breasts, cut into bite-sized pieces
Salt and pepper to taste
2 tablespoons olive oil
3 cloves garlic, minced
4 cups fresh spinach leaves
Zest of 1 lemon
Juice of 1 lemon
1/2 cup grated Parmesan cheese
Red pepper flakes (optional, for heat)

Instructions:

Cook the pasta according to the package instructions until al dente. Drain and set aside.
Season the chicken pieces with salt and pepper. Heat olive oil in a large skillet over medium-high heat. Add the chicken to the skillet and cook until browned and cooked through, about 6-8 minutes. Remove the chicken from the skillet and set aside.
In the same skillet, add minced garlic and sauté for 1-2 minutes until fragrant.
Add the spinach leaves to the skillet and cook until wilted, about 2-3 minutes.
Return the cooked chicken to the skillet with the spinach. Add the cooked pasta, lemon zest, and lemon juice. Toss everything together to combine.
Sprinkle the grated Parmesan cheese over the pasta and toss again until the cheese melts and coats the pasta evenly. If desired, add a pinch of red pepper flakes for some heat.
Taste and adjust the seasoning with salt and pepper if needed.
Remove from heat and serve the Chicken & Spinach Skillet Pasta with Lemon & Parmesan hot.
You can garnish with additional grated Parmesan and lemon wedges if desired.
Enjoy your delicious Chicken & Spinach Skillet Pasta with Lemon & Parmesan!

Quick-Cooking Oats

Ingredients:

1/2 cup quick-cooking oats
1 cup unsweetened almond milk (or any milk of your choice)
1/2 teaspoon cinnamon
1/4 teaspoon vanilla extract
1 tablespoon chopped nuts (such as almonds or walnuts)
1 tablespoon ground flaxseed (optional)
Fresh berries (such as blueberries or strawberries), for topping

Instructions:

In a small saucepan, combine the quick-cooking oats and almond milk. Bring to a boil over medium heat.
Reduce the heat to low and add the cinnamon and vanilla extract to the oats. Stir well to combine.
Cook the oats for about 1-2 minutes, stirring occasionally, until they reach your desired consistency. If you prefer thicker oats, cook for a bit longer.
Once the oats are cooked, remove the saucepan from the heat. Stir in the chopped nuts and ground flaxseed (if using). These additions add extra flavor, texture, and nutritional value.
Transfer the cooked oats to a serving bowl. Top with fresh berries or any other low-sugar fruits of your choice.
Allow the oats to cool slightly before enjoying.
This recipe provides a balanced combination of fiber, healthy fats, and protein from the oats, nuts, and flaxseed. It's a delicious and nutritious option for individuals with diabetes or those looking for a healthy breakfast choice.

Veggie & Hummus Sandwich

Ingredients:

2 slices whole-grain bread (look for low-carb or high-fiber options)
2 tablespoons hummus (choose a variety without added sugars)
1/4 cup thinly sliced cucumber
1/4 cup thinly sliced bell peppers (any color)
1/4 cup baby spinach leaves
1/4 small red onion, thinly sliced
Salt and pepper to taste

Instructions:

Spread hummus evenly on one side of each slice of bread.
Layer the cucumber slices, bell peppers, baby spinach, and red onion on top of one slice of bread.
Season the vegetables with a sprinkle of salt and pepper to taste.
Place the other slice of bread on top to create a sandwich.
Press the sandwich gently to help the ingredients stick together.
Slice the sandwich in half or quarters for easier handling, if desired.
Serve the Veggie & Hummus Sandwich immediately or wrap it up for later.
This recipe is packed with fresh vegetables and whole-grain bread, providing fiber, vitamins, and minerals while keeping the carbohydrate content in check. It's a satisfying and healthy option for individuals with diabetes. Feel free to customize the sandwich with additional vegetables or herbs based on your preferences.
Enjoy!

Avocado-Egg Toast

Ingredients:

1 slice whole-grain bread (look for low-carb or high-fiber options)
1/4 ripe avocado, mashed
1 hard-boiled egg, sliced
Salt and pepper to taste
Fresh herbs (such as cilantro or chives) for garnish (optional)

Instructions:

Toast the slice of whole-grain bread to your desired level of crispiness.
Spread the mashed avocado evenly on the toasted bread.
Arrange the sliced hard-boiled egg on top of the avocado.
Sprinkle with salt and pepper to taste. You can also add a pinch of your favorite herbs or spices for extra flavor.
Garnish with fresh herbs, if desired.
Serve the Avocado-Egg Toast as an open-faced sandwich or fold it in half for a more portable option.
This recipe offers a good balance of healthy fats, protein, and fiber from the avocado, egg, and whole-grain bread. It's a nutritious and diabetes-friendly choice for a quick breakfast or snack. Feel free to experiment with additional toppings such as cherry tomatoes, red pepper flakes, or a squeeze of lemon juice to customize the flavor.
Enjoy!

Peanut Butter Energy Balls

Ingredients:

1 cup old-fashioned oats
1/2 cup natural peanut butter (unsweetened, no added sugars)
1/4 cup ground flaxseed
1/4 cup unsweetened shredded coconut
1/4 cup chopped nuts (such as almonds or walnuts)
1/4 cup sugar-free honey or sugar substitute (such as stevia)
1 teaspoon vanilla extract
Pinch of salt

Instructions:

In a mixing bowl, combine the oats, peanut butter, ground flaxseed, shredded coconut, chopped nuts, sugar-free honey or sugar substitute, vanilla extract, and a pinch of salt. Stir well until all the ingredients are evenly combined.

Place the mixture in the refrigerator for about 15-30 minutes to allow it to firm up slightly, which will make it easier to roll into balls.

Once chilled, remove the mixture from the refrigerator. Take small portions of the mixture and roll them between your hands to form bite-sized energy balls. Repeat until all the mixture is used.

Place the energy balls on a plate or baking sheet lined with parchment paper. Refrigerate the energy balls for at least 1 hour to allow them to set.

Once set, the Peanut Butter Energy Balls are ready to be enjoyed. Store any leftovers in an airtight container in the refrigerator.

These Peanut Butter Energy Balls are a great snack option for individuals with diabetes. They provide a combination of healthy fats, fiber, and protein to help keep blood sugar levels stable. Remember to enjoy them in moderation as part of a balanced diet.

Turkey-Stuffed Bell Peppers

Ingredients:

4 large bell peppers (any color)
1 pound lean ground turkey
1 small onion, diced
2 cloves garlic, minced
1 cup cooked quinoa
1 can (14.5 ounces) diced tomatoes, drained
1 teaspoon dried oregano
1 teaspoon dried basil
Salt and pepper to taste
1/4 cup grated Parmesan cheese (optional)
Fresh parsley or cilantro for garnish (optional)

Instructions:

Preheat your oven to 375°F (190°C).
Cut the tops off the bell peppers and remove the seeds and membranes. Rinse the peppers thoroughly.
In a large skillet, cook the ground turkey over medium heat until browned. Drain any excess fat.
Add the diced onion and minced garlic to the skillet with the turkey. Cook for a few minutes until the onion is translucent.
Stir in the cooked quinoa, diced tomatoes, dried oregano, dried basil, salt, and pepper. Mix well to combine all the ingredients.
Stuff the bell peppers with the turkey-quinoa mixture, pressing it down gently.
Place the stuffed bell peppers upright in a baking dish. If the peppers are wobbly, you can slice a small piece off the bottom to create a flat surface.
Optional: Sprinkle grated Parmesan cheese on top of each stuffed bell pepper.
Cover the baking dish with foil and bake in the preheated oven for 30-35 minutes, or until the peppers are tender.
Remove the foil and bake for an additional 5 minutes to allow the cheese to melt and lightly brown.
Garnish with fresh parsley or cilantro, if desired.
Allow the Turkey-Stuffed Bell Peppes to cool slightly before serving.
These Turkey-Stuffed Bell Peppers are a nutritious and flavorful option for individuals with diabetes. They are low in carbohydrates and provide a good amount of protein and fiber. Enjoy them as a satisfying main dish or pair them with a side salad for a complete meal.

Tropical Chicken Cauliflower Rice Bowls

Ingredients:
For the Chicken:

2 boneless, skinless chicken breasts, cut into bite-sized pieces
1 tablespoon olive oil
2 cloves garlic, minced
1 teaspoon ground cumin
1 teaspoon paprika
Salt and pepper to taste

For the Cauliflower Rice:

1 medium head of cauliflower, riced (or 4 cups pre-riced cauliflower)
1 tablespoon coconut oil
1/4 cup diced red bell pepper
1/4 cup diced yellow bell pepper
1/4 cup diced red onion
1/4 cup diced pineapple
1/4 cup chopped cilantro (optional)
Juice of 1 lime
Salt and pepper to taste

For the Sauce:

1/4 cup unsweetened coconut milk
1 tablespoon low-sodium soy sauce or tamari
1 tablespoon lime juice
1 tablespoon natural peanut butter (unsweetened, no added sugars)
1/2 teaspoon grated fresh ginger
Pinch of red pepper flakes (optional, for heat)

Instructions:

In a bowl, combine the minced garlic, ground cumin, paprika, salt, and pepper. Add the chicken pieces and toss to coat them evenly with the spice mixture.

Heat olive oil in a skillet over medium-high heat. Add the seasoned chicken to the skillet and cook until browned and cooked through, about 6-8 minutes. Remove the chicken from the skillet and set aside.

In the same skillet, melt the coconut oil over medium heat. Add the diced red bell pepper, yellow bell pepper, and red onion. Sauté for about 3-4 minutes until the vegetables are slightly softened.

Add the riced cauliflower to the skillet and cook for an additional 4-5 minutes, stirring occasionally, until the cauliflower is tender.

Stir in the diced pineapple, chopped cilantro (if using), lime juice, salt, and pepper. Cook for another 1-2 minutes to allow the flavors to combine.

In a small bowl, whisk together the coconut milk, soy sauce or tamari, lime juice, peanut butter, grated ginger, and red pepper flakes (if using) to make the sauce.

Return the cooked chicken to the skillet with the cauliflower rice mixture. Pour the sauce over the ingredients and stir to coat everything evenly. Cook for another 1-2 minutes until everything is heated through.

Remove from heat and divide the Tropical Chicken Cauliflower Rice among serving bowls.

These Tropical Chicken Cauliflower Rice Bowls are packed with flavors and provide a balanced combination of lean protein, low-carb cauliflower rice, and colorful vegetables. They offer a healthy and satisfying option for individuals with diabetes. Enjoy the vibrant and delicious meal!

Slow-Cooker Pork Chops

Ingredients:

4 boneless pork chops (about 4 ounces each)
Salt and pepper to taste
1 tablespoon olive oil
1 small onion, thinly sliced
2 cloves garlic, minced
1 cup low-sodium chicken broth
1 tablespoon Dijon mustard
1 tablespoon low-sodium soy sauce or tamari
1 teaspoon dried thyme
1/2 teaspoon paprika
1/4 teaspoon red pepper flakes (optional, for heat)
2 tablespoons cornstarch (optional, for thickening)

Instructions:

Season the pork chops with salt and pepper to taste.

Heat olive oil in a skillet over medium-high heat. Add the pork chops and cook until browned on both sides, about 2-3 minutes per side. Remove the pok chops from the skillet and set aside.

In the same skillet, add the sliced onion and minced garlic. Sauté for about 2-3 minutes until the onion becomes translucent.
In a small bowl, whisk together the chicken broth, Dijon mustard, soy sauce or tamari, dried thyme, paprika, and red pepper flakes (if using).
Place the browned pork chops in the slow cooker. Pour the chicken broth mixture over the pork chops. Add the sautéed onions and garlic.
Cover the slow cooker and cook on low heat for 6-8 hours or on high heat for 3-4 hours, until the pork chops are tender and fully cooked.
If you prefer a thicker sauce, you can remove the pork chops from the slow cooker and transfer the sauce to a saucepan. Mix the cornstarch with a little water to create a slurry, then whisk it into the sauce. Heat the sauce on the stovetop over medium heat, stirring constantly, until it thickens.
Serve the Slow-Cooker Pork Chops with the sauce. You can garnish with fresh herbs such as parsley or chives if desired.
This recipe for Slow-Cooker Pork Chops is convenient and yields tender, flavorful pork chops. It's a diabetes-friendly option as it focuses on lean protein and utilizes low-sodium ingredients. Serve the pork chops with a side of non-starchy vegetables or a salad for a complete and balanced meal. Enjoy!

Sweet & Tangy Salmon with Green Beans

Ingredients:

2 salmon fillets (about 4-6 ounces each)
Salt and pepper to taste
2 tablespoons low-sodium soy sauce or tamari
2 tablespoons sugar-free honey or sugar substitute (such as stevia)
1 tablespoon rice vinegar
1 tablespoon freshly squeezed lemon juice
1 clove garlic, minced
1/2 teaspoon grated fresh ginger
1/2 pound fresh green beans, trimmed
1 tablespoon olive oil

Instructions:
Preheat your oven to 400°F (200°C).
Season the salmon fillets with salt and pepper to taste.
In a small bowl, whisk together the soy sauce or tamari, sugar-free honey or sugar substitute, rice vinegar, lemon juice, minced garlic, and grated ginger to make the sweet and tangy glaze.
Place the salmon fillets in a baking dish lined with parchment paper or aluminum foil.
Brush the glaze mixture evenly over the salmon fillets, reserving a small amount for later.
Bake the salmon in the preheated oven for about 12-15 minutes, or until the salmon is cooked to your desired level of doneness.
While the salmon is baking, heat olive oil in a skillet over medium heat. Add the green beans and sauté for about 5-7 minutes until they are tender-crisp.
Drizzle the remaining glaze over the sautéed green beans and toss them to coat evenly.
Serve the Sweet & Tangy Salmon alongside the glazed green beans.
This recipe provides a flavorful and diabetes-friendly option with the combination of omega-3-rich salmon and fresh green beans. The sweet and tangy glaze adds a delicious twist to the dish without adding excessive sugars. It's a balanced meal that is both nutritious and satisfying. Enjoy!

Spaghetti Squash Meatball Casserole

Ingredients:

1 medium-sized spaghetti squash
1 pound lean ground turkey or chicken
1/4 cup almond flour or breadcrumbs (choose a low-carb option if desired)
1/4 cup grated Parmesan cheese
1/4 cup chopped fresh parsley
1 clove garlic, minced
1/2 teaspoon dried oregano
1/2 teaspoon dried basil
1/2 teaspoon salt
1/4 teaspoon black pepper
1 cup low-sugar marinara sauce
1/2 cup shredded mozzarella cheese
Fresh basil leaves for garnish (optional)

Instructions:

Preheat your oven to 375°F (190°C).
Cut the spaghetti squash in half lengthwise. Scoop out the seeds and pulp with a spoon.
Place the spaghetti squash halves cut-side down on a baking sheet lined with parchment paper. Bake in the preheated oven for about 40-45 minutes, or until the squash is tender and the strands can easily be scraped out with a fork. Set aside.
In a mixing bowl, combine the ground turkey or chicken, almond flour or breadcrumbs, grated Parmesan cheese, chopped parsley, minced garlic, dried oregano, dried basil, salt, and black pepper. Mix well until all the ingredients are evenly combined.
Shape the mixture into small meatballs, about 1 inch in diameter.
Heat a non-stick skillet over medium heat. Add the meatballs and cook until browned on all sides, about 6-8 minutes. Make sure the meatballs are cooked through.
In a casserole dish, spread a thin layer of marinara sauce on the bottom.
Using a fork, scrape the spaghetti squash strands into the casserole dish, creating a layer of "spaghetti".
Place the cooked meatballs on top of the spaghetti squash.
Pour the remaining marinara sauce over the meatballs.
Sprinkle the shredded mozzarella cheese on top of the casserole.
Bake in the oven for about 15-20 minutes, or until the cheese is melted and bubbly.
Remove from the oven and let it cool slightly before serving.
Garnish with fresh basil leaves, if desired.
This Spaghetti Squash Meatball Casserole offers a low-carb alternative to traditional pasta dishes. The spaghetti squash provides a fiber-rich base, while the lean turkey or chicken meatballs offer protein without excessive saturated fats. It's a diabetes-friendly recipe that is both flavorful and satisfying. Enjoy!

Parmesan Chicken with Artichoke Hearts

Ingredients:

4 boneless, skinless chicken breasts
Salt and pepper to taste
1/4 cup grated Parmesan cheese
1/4 cup almond flour or breadcrumbs
(choose a low-carb option if desired)
1 teaspoon dried basil
1 teaspoon dried oregano
1/2 teaspoon garlic powder
1 tablespoon olive oil
1 can (14 ounces) artichoke hearts, drained and chopped
1/4 cup diced red onion
2 cloves garlic, minced
1 tablespoon lemon juice
1/4 cup low-sodium chicken broth
1/4 cup shredded mozzarella cheese
Fresh parsley for garnish (optional)

Instructions:

Preheat your oven to 400°F (200°C).
Season the chicken breasts with salt and pepper to taste.
In a shallow dish, combine the grated Parmesan cheese, almond flour or breadcrumbs, dried basil, dried oregano, and garlic powder.
Dip each chicken breast into the Parmesan mixture, pressing it firmly to coat both sides.
Heat olive oil in an oven-safe skillet over medium-high heat. Add the coated chicken breasts to the skillet and cook for about 3-4 minutes per side, or until they are golden brown.
Remove the skillet from the heat and transfer the chicken breasts to a plate. Set aside.
In the same skillet, add the chopped artichoke hearts, diced red onion, minced garlic, lemon juice, and chicken broth. Stir well to combine.
Place the cooked chicken breasts back into the skillet, on top of the artichoke mixture.
Sprinkle the shredded mozzarella cheese evenly over the chicken breasts.
Transfer the skillet to the preheated oven and bake for about 15-20 minutes, or until the chicken is cooked through and the cheese is melted and lightly browned.
Remove from the oven and let it cool slightly.
Garnish with fresh parsley, if desired, before serving.
This Parmesan Chicken with Artichoke Hearts rcipe offers a delicious and diabetes-friendly option. The chicken breasts are coated in a flavorful Parmesan mixture and then topped with artichoke hearts and cheese for added texture and taste. Serve it with a side of steamed vegetables or a fresh salad for a complete and balanced meal. Enjoy!

Salmon & Spinach Salad with Avocado

Ingredients:

2 salmon fillets (about 4-6 ounces each)
Salt and pepper to taste
4 cups fresh baby spinach
1 ripe avocado, sliced
1/4 cup cherry tomatoes, halved
1/4 cup thinly sliced red onion
2 tablespoons chopped fresh dill (optional)
Juice of 1 lemon
1 tablespoon extra-virgin olive oil

Instructions:

Preheat your oven to 400°F (200°C).
Season the salmon fillets with salt and pepper to taste.
Place the salmon fillets on a baking sheet lined with parchment paper or aluminum foil. Bake in the preheated oven for about 12-15 minutes, or until the salmon is cooked to your desired level of doneness.
Remove from the oven and let it cool slightly.
In a large salad bowl, add the baby spinach, avocado slices, cherry tomatoes, and thinly sliced red onion.
Flake the cooked salmon into bite-sized pieces and add it to the salad bowl.
In a small bowl, whisk together the lemon juice and extra-virgin olive oil to create the dressing.
Drizzle the dressing over the salad and gently toss to coat all the ingredients.
Sprinkle with chopped fresh dill, if desired.
This Salmon & Spinach Salad with Avocado is a refreshing and nutritious option. It combines omega-3-rich salmon, nutrient-dense spinach, and creamy avocado for a well-rounded meal. The dressing adds a burst of flavor without added sugars. Enjoy this vibrant and diabetes-friendly salad as a light lunch or dinner.

Shrimp Avocado Salad

Ingredients:

1 pound cooked shrimp, peeled and deveined
2 ripe avocados, diced
1 cup cherry tomatoes, halved
1/4 cup diced red onion
1/4 cup chopped fresh cilantro
Juice of 1 lime
1 tablespoon extra-virgin olive oil
Salt and pepper to taste
Optional: additional lime wedges and fresh cilantro for garnish

Instructions:

In a large mixing bowl, combine the cooked shrimp, diced avocados, cherry tomatoes, diced red onion, and chopped cilantro.
In a separate small bowl, whisk together the lime juice and extra-virgin olive oil to make the dressing.
Drizzle the dressing over the shrimp and avocado mixture. Gently toss to coat all the ingredients. Season with salt and pepper to taste.
Let the salad sit for a few minutes to allow the flavors to meld together.
Serve the Shrimp Avocado Salad in individual bowls or plates.
Optional: Garnish with additional lime wedges and fresh cilantro for extra freshness and presentation.
This Shrimp Avocado Salad is a light and refreshing option that offers a good balance of protein, healthy fats, and fresh vegetables. The lime dressing adds a tangy kick without added sugars. It's a satisfying and diabetes-friendly choice for a quick and nutritious meal. Enjoy!

Sheet-Pan Chicken and Vegetables

Ingredients:

4 boneless, skinless chicken breasts
Salt and pepper to taste
2 tablespoons olive oil, divided
1 tablespoon Dijon mustard
1 tablespoon lemon juice
2 cloves garlic, minced
1 teaspoon dried thyme
1/2 teaspoon paprika
1/2 teaspoon onion powder
1/2 teaspoon dried rosemary
1/2 pound baby potatoes, halved or quartered
2 cups broccoli florets
1 red bell pepper, sliced
1 yellow bell pepper, sliced
1 medium zucchini, sliced

Instructions:

Preheat your oven to 425°F (220°C).

Season the chicken breasts with salt and pepper to taste.
In a small bowl, whisk together 1 tablespoon of olive oil, Dijon mustard, lemon juice, minced garlic, dried thyme, paprika, onion powder, and dried rosemary to make the marinade.
Place the chicken breasts in a large resealable bag and pour the marinade over them. Seal the bag and massage the marinade into the chicken breasts. Let them marinate in the refrigerator for at least 30 minutes or up to overnight.
In a large bowl, combine the halved baby potatoes, broccoli florets, sliced bell peppers, and sliced zucchini. Drizzle with the remaining 1 tablespoon of olive oil and season with salt and pepper. Toss to coat the vegetables evenly.
Line a baking sheet with parchment paper or lightly grease it. Arrange the marinated chicken breasts on one side of the baking sheet and the seasoned vegetables on the other side.
Bake in the preheated oven for about 25-30 minutes, or until the chicken is cooked through and the vegetables are tender and lightly browned. The internal temperature of the chicken should reach 165°F (74°C).
Remove the sheet pan from the oven and let it cool for a few minutes.
Serve the Sheet-Pan Chicken and Vegetables as is or with a side of quinoa or brown rice for a complete meal.
This Sheet-Pan Chicken and Vegetables recipe is a convenient and diabetes-friendly option as it combines lean protein and a variety of colorful vegetables. The marinade adds flavor without excessive sugars or unhealthy fats. It's an easy and wholesome dish that can be customized with your favorite vegetables. Enjoy!

Spicy Beef & Pepper Stir-Fry

Ingredients:

1 pound beef sirloin, thinly sliced
2 tablespoons low-sodium soy sauce
1 tablespoon rice vinegar
1 tablespoon cornstarch
1 tablespoon sesame oil
2 cloves garlic, minced
1 teaspoon grated fresh ginger
1/2 teaspoon red pepper flakes (adjust to your desired level of spiciness)
1 red bell pepper, thinly sliced
1 green bell pepper, thinly sliced
1 yellow bell pepper, thinly sliced
1 medium onion, thinly sliced
2 tablespoons low-sodium beef broth
1 tablespoon low-sodium hoisin sauce
1 tablespoon sriracha sauce (optional)
2 green onions, chopped (for garnish)
Sesame seeds (for garnish)
Cooking spray or a small amount of vegetable oil for cooking

Instructions:

In a bowl, combine the thinly sliced beef, soy sauce, rice vinegar, cornstarch, and sesame oil. Toss to coat the beef evenly. Set aside to marinate for about 10-15 minutes.

Heat a large skillet or wok over medium-high heat. Lightly coat the skillet with cooking spray or a small amount of vegetable oil.

Add the minced garlic, grated ginger, and red pepper flakes to the skillet. Stir-fry for about 1 minute until fragrant.

Add the marinated beef to the skillet and stir-fry for about 3-4 minutes, or until the beef is browned and cooked through. Transfer the cooked beef to a plate and set aside.

In the same skillet, add the sliced bell peppers and onion. Stir-fry for about 3-4 minutes, or until the vegetables are crisp-tender.

In a small bowl, whisk together the beef broth, hoisin sauce, and sriracha sauce (if using). Pour the sauce mixture into the skillet with the cooked vegetables. Stir to coat the vegetables evenly.

Return the cooked beef to the skillet and toss to combine with the vegetables and sauce. Cook for an additional 1-2 minutes to heat through.

Remove the skillet from the heat.

Serve the Spicy Beef & Pepper Stir-Fry hot, garnished with chopped green onions and sesame seeds.

This Spicy Beef & Pepper Stir-Fry recipe offers a flavorful combination of tender beef, vibrant bell peppers, and a spicy sauce. The use of low-sodium soy sauce and hoisin sauce helps to control sodium levels. It's a satisfying and diabetes-friendly dish that can be served with steamed brown rice or cauliflower rice for a complete meal. Enjoy!

Pulled Chicken Sandwiches

Ingredients:

4 boneless, skinless chicken breasts
1 cup low-sodium chicken broth
1/2 cup tomato sauce
1/4 cup apple cider vinegar
2 tablespoons honey or a sugar substitute (optional)
1 tablespoon Worcestershire sauce
1 tablespoon Dijon mustard
1 teaspoon garlic powder
1 teaspoon onion powder
1/2 teaspoon smoked paprika
1/2 teaspoon chili powder
1/4 teaspoon cayenne pepper (optional, adjust to your desired level of spiciness)
Salt and pepper to taste
4 whole wheat or whole grain buns
Optional toppings: sliced tomatoes, lettuce, red onion, pickles

Instructions:

In a slow cooker, combine the chicken broth, tomato sauce, apple cider vinegar, honey or sugar substitute (if using), Worcestershire sauce, Dijon mustard, garlic powder, onion powder, smoked paprika, chili powder, cayenne pepper (if using), salt, and pepper. Stir well to combine.
Add the chicken breasts to the slow cooker, ensuring they are fully submerged in the liquid.
Cover the slow cooker and cook on low heat for 6-8 hours or on high heat for 3-4 hours, or until the chicken is tender and easily shredded.
Once the chicken is cooked, remove it from the slow cooker and shred it using two forks.
Optional step: If you prefer a thicker sauce, transfer the cooking liquid from the slow cooker to a saucepan and simmer over medium heat until it reduces and thickens slightly.
Return the shredded chicken to the slow cooker or saucepan with the reduced sauce. Stir to coat the chicken evenly.
Serve the pulled chicken on whole wheat or whole grain buns. Add your preferred toppings such as sliced tomatoes, lettuce, red onion, or pickles.
This Pulled Chicken Sandwich recipe provides a diabetes-friendly twist on the classic barbecue sandwich. The homemade sauce is tangy and flavorful, and you have the option to adjust the level of sweetness and spiciness according to your preference. Enjoy this delicious and satisfying meal while keeping your blood sugar levels in check.

Skillet Pork Chops with Apples & Onion

Ingredients:

4 boneless pork chops (about 4 ounces each), trimmed of excess fat
1 tablespoon olive oil
1 medium onion, thinly sliced
2 medium apples (such as Granny Smith or Honeycrisp), cored and thinly sliced
1/2 teaspoon ground cinnamon
1/4 teaspoon ground nutmeg
Salt and pepper to taste
1/2 cup low-sodium chicken broth
Fresh parsley for garnish (optional)

Instructions:

Season the pork chops with salt and pepper on both sides.
Heat the olive oil in a large skillet over medium-high heat. Add the pork chops and cook for about 3-4 minutes per side until browned. Remove the pork chops from the skillet and set them aside.
In the same skillet, add the sliced onion and cook over medium heat until softened and lightly browned, stirring occasionally. This should take about 5 minutes.
Add the sliced apples, cinnamon, nutmeg, salt, and pepper to the skillet. Stir everything together and cook for another 3-4 minutes until the apples are slightly tender.
Pour the chicken broth into the skillet and bring it to a simmer. Return the pork chops to the skillet, cover, and let them cook for about 6-8 minutes or until the chops are cooked through and reach an internal temperature of 145°F (63°C).
Once cooked, remove the skillet from the heat. Let the pork chops rest for a couple of minutes before serving.
Serve the skillet pork chops with the apples and onion mixture spooned over the top. Garnish with fresh parsley if desired.
This recipe provides a delicious combination of flavors with the savory pork chops and the sweet-tart apples. Remember to adjust the portion sizes and ingredients based on your specific dietary needs and consult with a healthcare professional or registered dietitian for personalized advice. Enjoy your meal!

Ginger Steak Fried Rice

Ingredients:

8 ounces lean steak (such as sirloin or flank steak), thinly sliced
1 tablespoon low-sodium soy sauce
1 tablespoon rice vinegar
2 teaspoons grated fresh ginger
2 garlic cloves, minced
1 tablespoon canola oil
2 cups cooked brown rice, chilled
1 cup mixed vegetables (such as peas, carrots, and bell peppers)
2 green onions, thinly sliced
2 large eggs, beaten
Salt and pepper to taste
Optional toppings: sesame seeds, chopped cilantro

Instructions:

In a bowl, combine the soy sauce, rice vinegar, grated ginger, and minced garlic. Add the thinly sliced steak to the bowl and let it marinate for about 10-15 minutes.
Heat the canola oil in a large skillet or wok over medium-high heat. Add the marinated steak (reserving the marinade) and cook for about 2-3 minutes until the steak is browned and cooked to your desired level of doneness. Remove the steak from the skillet and set it aside.
In the same skillet, add the chilled cooked rice and mixed vegetables. Stir-fry for about 3-4 minutes until the vegetables are tender and the rice is heated through.
Push the rice and vegetables to one side of the skillet and pour the beaten eggs into the empty space. Scramble the eggs until they are cooked, breaking them into small pieces.
Add the cooked steak back to the skillet with the rice and vegetables. Pour the reserved marinade over the ingredients in the skillet. Stir everything together and cook for another 1-2 minutes to heat everything through.
Season with salt and pepper to taste. Stir in the sliced green onions.
Remove the skillet from the heat and divide the ginger steak fried rice into serving bowls. Sprinkle with sesame seeds and chopped cilantro as optional toppings.
Enjoy this flavorful and satisfying ginger steak fried rice! Remember to adjust the portion sizes and ingredients based on your specific dietary needs and consult with a healthcare professional or registered dietitian for personalized advice.

Grilled Beef Chimichangas

Ingredients:

1 pound lean ground beef
1 small onion, finely chopped
2 cloves garlic, minced
1 teaspoon ground cumin
1 teaspoon chili powder
1/2 teaspoon dried oregano
Salt and pepper to taste
4 whole wheat tortillas (8-inch size)
1 cup shredded reduced-fat cheese (such as cheddar or Monterey Jack)
1/4 cup chopped fresh cilantro
Salsa, guacamole, or sour cream for serving (optional)

Instructions:

Preheat your grill to medium heat.
In a skillet over medium-high heat, cook the ground beef, onion, and garlic until the beef is browned and the onion is softened. Break up the beef into small crumbles as it cooks.
Drain any excess fat from the skillet. Add the ground cumin, chili powder, dried oregano, salt, and pepper to the skillet. Stir to combine and cook for an additional 2-3 minutes to allow the flavors to meld. Remove from heat.
Lay out the whole wheat tortillas and divide the beef mixture evenly among them, placing it in the center of each tortilla. Sprinkle shredded cheese and chopped cilantro on top of the beef mixture.
Fold the sides of each tortilla inward, then roll up tightly to form a chimichanga. Secure the edges with toothpicks if needed.
Place the chimichangas on the preheated grill and cook for about 4-5 minutes per side, or until they are crispy and heated through.
Remove the chimichangas from the grill and let them cool slightly. Remove the toothpicks if used.
Serve the grilled beef chimichangas with salsa, guacamole, or sour cream if desired. You can also add a side of mixed greens or a salad for a complete meal.
Enjoy these delicious grilled beef chimichangas! Remember to adjust the portion sizes and ingredients based on your specific dietary needs and consult with a healthcare professional or registered dietitian for personalized advice.

Power Lasagna

Ingredients:

9 whole wheat lasagna noodles
1 pound lean ground turkey or chicken
1 medium onion, finely chopped
2 cloves garlic, minced
1 medium zucchini, grated
1 cup sliced mushrooms
1 can (14 ounces) crushed tomatoes
1 can (6 ounces) tomato paste
1 teaspoon dried basil
1 teaspoon dried oregano
Salt and pepper to taste
1 cup low-fat ricotta cheese
1/2 cup grated Parmesan cheese
2 cups fresh spinach leaves
1 cup shredded part-skim mozzarella cheese

Instructions:

Preheat the oven to 375°F (190°C). Prepare a 9x13-inch baking dish by lightly greasing it with cooking spray.
Cook the lasagna noodles according to the package instructions until al dente. Drain the noodles and set them aside.
In a large skillet, cook the ground turkey or chicken over medium heat until browned. Add the onion, garlic, grated zucchini, and sliced mushrooms to the skillet. Cook for an additional 5 minutes, or until the vegetables have softened.
Stir in the crushed tomatoes, tomato paste, dried basil, dried oregano, salt, and pepper. Simmer the sauce for about 10-15 minutes to allow the flavors to blend.
In a separate bowl, combine the ricotta cheese and grated Parmesan cheese. Mix well.
To assemble the lasagna, spread a thin layer of the meat sauce on the bottom of the prepared baking dish. Place three lasagna noodles on top of the sauce.
Spread half of the ricotta cheese mixture over the noodles, followed by half of the fresh spinach leaves. Top with a layer of the meat sauce.
Repeat the layers with three more lasagna noodles, the remaining ricotta cheese mixture, the remaining spinach leaves, and another layer of the meat sauce.
Finish with a final layer of three lasagna noodles and the remaining meat sauce. Sprinkle the shredded mozzarella cheese evenly over the top.
Cover the baking dish with foil and bake in the preheated oven for 30 minutes. Then, remove the foil and continue baking for an additional 15 minutes, or until the cheese is melted and bubbly.
Remove the lasagna from the oven and let it cool for a few minutes before serving.
Serve the Power Lasagna with a side salad or steamed vegetables for a balanced meal. Remember to adjust the portion sizes and ingredients based on your specific dietary needs and consult with a healthcare professional or registered dietitian for personalized advice. Enjoy!

Simple Sesame Chicken with Couscous

Ingredients:

4 boneless, skinless chicken breasts (about 4 ounces each)
2 tablespoons low-sodium soy sauce
1 tablespoon honey
2 teaspoons toasted sesame oil
2 teaspoons grated fresh ginger
2 cloves garlic, minced
2 tablespoons sesame seeds
Salt and pepper to taste
1 cup whole wheat couscous
1 ¼ cups low-sodium chicken broth
2 green onions, thinly sliced

Instructions:

Preheat the oven to 400°F (200°C).
In a small bowl, whisk together the soy sauce, honey, toasted sesame oil, grated ginger, minced garlic, and sesame seeds.
Season the chicken breasts with salt and pepper. Place them in a baking dish and pour the sauce mixture over the chicken, making sure it is evenly coated. Reserve a small amount of the sauce for later.
Bake the chicken in the preheated oven for about 20-25 minutes or until the chicken is cooked through and no longer pink in the center.
While the chicken is baking, prepare the couscous according to the package instructions, using the low-sodium chicken broth instead of water.
Fluff the cooked couscous with a fork and stir in the thinly sliced green onions.
Once the chicken is done, remove it from the oven and let it rest for a few minutes. Slice the chicken into strips.
Serve the sesame chicken over the cooked couscous. Drizzle the reserved sauce over the chicken and couscous for extra flavor.
Enjoy this simple and flavorful sesame chicken with couscous! Remember to adjust the portion sizes and ingredients based on your specific dietary needs and consult with a healthcare professional or registered dietitian for personalized advice.

Braised Pork Stew

Ingredients:

1 ½ pounds boneless pork shoulder, trimmed of excess fat and cut into 1-inch cubes
1 tablespoon olive oil
1 medium onion, chopped
2 cloves garlic, minced
2 medium carrots, peeled and sliced
2 celery stalks, sliced
1 cup low-sodium chicken broth
1 cup water
1 can (14 ounces) diced tomatoes (no added salt)
1 teaspoon dried thyme
1 bay leaf
Salt and pepper to taste
2 cups chopped fresh spinach

Instructions:

Heat the olive oil in a large pot or Dutch oven over medium-high heat. Add the pork cubes and brown them on all sides. Remove the pork from the pot and set it aside.
In the same pot, add the chopped onion and minced garlic. Sauté for a few minutes until the onion is translucent and fragrant.
Add the sliced carrots and celery to the pot. Cook for another 3-4 minutes until the vegetables start to soften.
Return the browned pork to the pot. Pour in the low-sodium chicken broth, water, and diced tomatoes (with their juices). Add the dried thyme, bay leaf, salt, and pepper. Stir to combine.
Bring the mixture to a boil, then reduce the heat to low. Cover the pot and let the stew simmer for about 1 ½ to 2 hours, or until the pork is tender and easily falls apart.
In the last 10 minutes of cooking, stir in the chopped fresh spinach. Let it wilt into the stew.
Remove the bay leaf from the stew before serving.
Serve the braised pork stew hot and enjoy! You can pair it with a side of steamed vegetables or a small portion of whole grain bread, if desired. Remember to adjust the portion sizes and ingredients based on your specific dietary needs and consult with a healthcare professional or registered dietitian for personalized advice.

Beef & Rice Stuffed Cabbage Rolls

Ingredients:

8 large cabbage leaves
1 pound lean ground beef
1 small onion, finely chopped
1 clove garlic, minced
1/2 cup cooked brown rice
1/4 cup chopped fresh parsley
1/2 teaspoon dried thyme
1/2 teaspoon paprika
Salt and pepper to taste
1 can (14 ounces) low-sodium diced tomatoes
1 cup low-sodium beef broth
1 tablespoon tomato paste

Instructions:

Preheat the oven to 350°F (175°C). Lightly grease a baking dish with cooking spray.
Bring a large pot of water to a boil. Add the cabbage leaves and blanch them for about 3-4 minutes, or until they are slightly softened. Drain the leaves and set them aside to cool.
In a skillet over medium heat, cook the ground beef, onion, and garlic until the beef is browned and the onion is softened. Break up the beef into small crumbles as it cooks.
Drain any excess fat from the skillet. Stir in the cooked brown rice, chopped parsley, dried thyme, paprika, salt, and pepper. Mix well.
Place a spoonful of the beef and rice mixture in the center of each cabbage leaf. Roll the leaf, tucking in the sides as you go, to form a tight roll. Repeat with the remaining cabbage leaves and filling.
Place the stuffed cabbage rolls in the greased baking dish, seam side down.
In a bowl, whisk together the diced tomatoes, beef broth, and tomato paste. Pour the tomato mixture over the cabbage rolls in the baking dish.
Cover the baking dish with foil and bake in the preheated oven for about 45 minutes to 1 hour, or until the cabbage rolls are tender.
Remove the foil and continue baking for an additional 10-15 minutes to allow the tops to brown slightly.
Remove the stuffed cabbage rolls from the oven and let them cool for a few minutes before serving.
Serve the beef and rice stuffed cabbage rolls with a side of steamed vegetables or a fresh salad for a complete meal. Remember to adjust the portion sizes and ingredients based on your specific dietary needs and consult with a healthcare professional or registered dietitian for personalized advice. Enjoy!

Meaty Slow-Cooked Jambalaya

Ingredients:

1 pound boneless, skinless chicken breasts, cut into 1-inch pieces
1/2 pound turkey sausage, sliced
1 large onion, chopped
1 green bell pepper, chopped
1 red bell pepper, chopped
2 celery stalks, chopped
3 cloves garlic, minced
1 can (14 ounces) diced tomatoes (no added salt)
1 cup low-sodium chicken broth
1 cup uncooked brown rice
1 tablespoon Cajun seasoning (look for a low-sodium option)
1/2 teaspoon dried thyme
1/2 teaspoon dried oregano
1/2 teaspoon paprika
Salt and pepper to taste
Chopped fresh parsley for garnish (optional)

Instructions:

In a large skillet, brown the chicken pieces and turkey sausage over medium-high heat. Remove them from the skillet and set them aside.
In the same skillet, add the chopped onion, green bell pepper, red bell pepper, celery, and minced garlic. Sauté for about 5 minutes until the vegetables are softened.
Transfer the sautéed vegetables to a slow cooker. Add the browned chicken and turkey sausage to the slow cooker as well.
Add the diced tomatoes (with their juices), chicken broth, uncooked brown rice, Cajun seasoning, dried thyme, dried oregano, paprika, salt, and pepper to the slow cooker. Stir well to combine all the ingredients.
Cover the slow cooker and cook on low heat for 4-6 hours, or until the chicken is cooked through and the rice is tender.
Stir the jambalaya before serving. Taste and adjust the seasoning if needed.
Serve the meaty slow-cooked jambalaya hot, garnished with chopped fresh parsley if desired.
Enjoy this flavorful meaty jambalaya! Remember to adjust the portion sizes and ingredients based on your specific dietary needs and consult with a healthcare professional or registered dietitian for personalized advice.

Slow Cooker Boeuf Bourguignon

Ingredients:

2 pounds lean beef stew meat, cut into 1-inch cubes
1 tablespoon olive oil
1 medium onion, chopped
2 cloves garlic, minced
2 carrots, peeled and sliced
8 ounces mushrooms, quartered
1 cup low-sodium beef broth
1 cup dry red wine (such as Burgundy or Pinot Noir)
2 tablespoons tomato paste
1 teaspoon dried thyme
1 bay leaf
Salt and pepper to taste
1 tablespoon cornstarch (optional, for thickening)
Chopped fresh parsley for garnish (optional)

Instructions:

Heat the olive oil in a large skillet over medium-high heat. Add the beef stew meat in batches and brown it on all sides. Transfer the browned beef to a slow cooker.
In the same skillet, add the chopped onion, minced garlic, sliced carrots, and quartered mushrooms. Sauté for a few minutes until the vegetables are slightly softened.
Transfer the sautéed vegetables to the slow cooker with the beef.
In a separate bowl, whisk together the beef broth, red wine, tomato paste, dried thyme, bay leaf, salt, and pepper. Pour this mixture over the beef and vegetables in the slow cooker. Stir to combine.
Cover the slow cooker and cook on low heat for 6-8 hours, or until the beef is tender.
In the last 30 minutes of cooking, you can thicken the sauce if desired. In a small bowl, mix the cornstarch with a few tablespoons of water to make a slurry. Stir the slurry into the slow cooker and let it cook for an additional 30 minutes until the sauce thickens.
Remove the bay leaf from the slow cooker before serving.
Serve the slow cooker boeuf bourguignon hot, garnished with chopped fresh parsley if desired. It pairs well with steamed vegetables or a side of cauliflower mash for a complete meal.
Enjoy this delicious slow cooker boeuf bourguignon! Remember to adjust the portion sizes and ingredients based on your specific dietary needs and consult with a healthcare professional or registered dietitian for personalized advice.

Saucy Pork Chop Skillet

Ingredients:

4 boneless pork chops, about 4 ounces each
1 tablespoon olive oil
1 medium onion, sliced
2 cloves garlic, minced
1 red bell pepper, sliced
1 green bell pepper, sliced
1 can (14 ounces) diced tomatoes (no added salt)
1 can (6 ounces) tomato paste
1 teaspoon dried oregano
1/2 teaspoon dried basil
1/2 teaspoon paprika
Salt and pepper to taste
Chopped fresh parsley for garnish (optional)

Instructions:

Season the pork chops with salt and pepper. In a large skillet, heat the olive oil over medium-high heat. Add the pork chops to the skillet and cook for about 3-4 minutes per side, or until browned. Remove the pork chops from the skillet and set them aside.
In the same skillet, add the sliced onion, minced garlic, red bell pepper, and green bell pepper. Sauté for about 5 minutes, or until the vegetables are slightly softened.
Stir in the diced tomatoes (with their juices), tomato paste, dried oregano, dried basil, paprika, salt, and pepper. Mix well to combine the ingredients.
Return the pork chops to the skillet, nestling them into the tomato and vegetable mixture.
Reduce the heat to low, cover the skillet, and let it simmer for about 15-20 minutes, or until the pork chops are cooked through and tender.
Remove the skillet from the heat. Sprinkle the saucy pork chops with chopped fresh parsley if desired.
Serve the saucy pork chops hot, spooning the tomato and vegetable sauce over them. It pairs well with steamed vegetables or a side of quinoa or brown rice.
Enjoy this flavorful saucy pork chop skillet! Remember to adjust the portion sizes and ingredients based on your specific dietary needs and consult with a healthcare professional or registered dietitian for personalized advice.

Marinated Steak & Pepper Fajitas

Ingredients:

1 pound flank steak, thinly sliced
2 bell peppers (red, green, or a combination), thinly sliced
1 medium onion, thinly sliced
2 cloves garlic, minced
2 tablespoons olive oil
2 tablespoons lime juice
1 tablespoon low-sodium soy sauce
1 teaspoon ground cumin
1 teaspoon chili powder
Salt and pepper to taste
Whole wheat tortillas, for serving
Optional toppings: salsa, Greek yogurt (as a sour cream substitute), chopped fresh cilantro

Instructions:

In a bowl, whisk together the olive oil, lime juice, low-sodium soy sauce, minced garlic, ground cumin, chili powder, salt, and pepper to make the marinade.
Place the sliced flank steak in a resealable plastic bag or a shallow dish. Pour the marinade over the steak, making sure it is evenly coated. Let the steak marinate in the refrigerator for at least 30 minutes, or up to overnight for maximum flavor.
Preheat a grill or a skillet over medium-high heat. If using a skillet, add a little olive oil to prevent sticking.
Remove the marinated steak from the refrigerator and drain off any excess marinade. Discard the remaining marinade.
Cook the steak slices on the preheated grill or skillet for about 3-4 minutes per side, or until they reach your desired level of doneness. Remove the cooked steak from the heat and let it rest for a few minutes.
In the same skillet or on the grill, add the sliced bell peppers and onion. Cook for about 5-6 minutes, or until the vegetables are softened and slightly charred.
Slice the cooked steak into thin strips, against the grain.
Warm the whole wheat tortillas according to package instructions.
Assemble the fajitas by placing some steak slices and cooked peppers and onions on each tortilla. Add your desired toppings such as salsa, Greek yogurt, or chopped fresh cilantro.
Roll up the tortillas tightly and serve the marinated steak and pepper fajitas warm.
Enjoy these delicious marinated steak and pepper fajitas! Remember to adjust the portion sizes and ingredients based on your specific dietary needs and consult with a healthcare professional or registered dietitian for personalized advice.

Asian Turkey Lettuce Cups

Ingredients:

1 pound ground turkey
1 tablespoon sesame oil
1 tablespoon low-sodium soy sauce
2 cloves garlic, minced
1 teaspoon minced ginger
1 small onion, finely chopped
1 bell pepper, finely chopped
2 green onions, sliced
2 tablespoons hoisin sauce
1 tablespoon rice vinegar
1 teaspoon sriracha sauce (optional, adjust to taste)
Salt and pepper to taste
Iceberg lettuce leaves, for serving
Optional toppings: shredded carrots, chopped peanuts, chopped fresh cilantro

Instructions:

Heat the sesame oil in a large skillet or wok over medium-high heat. Add the ground turkey and cook, breaking it up with a spoon, until it is browned and cooked through.
Add the minced garlic, minced ginger, and chopped onion to the skillet. Sauté for a few minutes until the onion is translucent and the garlic and ginger are fragrant.
Stir in the chopped bell pepper and sliced green onions. Cook for another 2-3 minutes until the bell pepper is slightly softened.
In a small bowl, whisk together the low-sodium soy sauce, hoisin sauce, rice vinegar, sriracha sauce (if using), salt, and pepper. Pour the sauce mixture over the turkey and vegetable mixture in the skillet. Stir well to coat everything evenly.
Reduce the heat to low and let the mixture simmer for a few minutes, allowing the flavors to meld together.
Wash and separate the iceberg lettuce leaves, using them as cups to hold the filling.
Spoon the Asian turkey mixture into the lettuce cups.
Top the lettuce cups with optional toppings such as shredded carrots, chopped peanuts, and chopped fresh cilantro.
Serve the Asian turkey lettuce cups as a light and flavorful meal.
Enjoy these tasty Asian turkey lettuce cups! Remember to adjust the portion sizes and ingredients based on your specific dietary needs and consult with a healthcare professional or registered dietitian for personalized advice.

Steak San Marino

Ingredients:

1 pound sirloin steak, about 1-inch thick
1 tablespoon olive oil
2 cloves garlic, minced
1/4 cup low-sodium soy sauce
2 tablespoons balsamic vinegar
1 tablespoon Dijon mustard
1 teaspoon dried oregano
1/2 teaspoon black pepper
Salt to taste
Chopped fresh parsley for garnish (optional)

Instructions:

In a small bowl, whisk together the minced garlic, low-sodium soy sauce, balsamic vinegar, Dijon mustard, dried oregano, black pepper, and a pinch of salt.

Place the sirloin steak in a shallow dish and pour the marinade over it. Make sure the steak is well coated on all sides. Cover the dish and let the steak marinate in the refrigerator for at least 30 minutes, or up to 4 hours for maximum flavor.

Preheat a grill or a skillet over medium-high heat. If using a skillet, add a little olive oil to prevent sticking.

Remove the marinated steak from the refrigerator and drain off any excess marinade. Discard the remaining marinade.

Cook the steak on the preheated grill or skillet for about 4-5 minutes per side, or until it reaches your desired level of doneness. The cooking time may vary depending on the thickness of the steak and your preferred doneness. For medium-rare, the internal temperature should reach 135°F (57°C).

Remove the steak from the heat and let it rest for a few minutes before slicing.

Slice the cooked steak against the grain into thin strips.

Serve the Steak San Marino hot, garnished with chopped fresh parsley if desired. It pairs well with steamed vegetables or a side of quinoa or roasted potatoes.

Chicken with Celery Root Puree

Ingredients:

4 boneless, skinless chicken breasts
1 tablespoon olive oil
Salt and pepper to taste
1 celery root (celeriac), peeled and diced
2 medium potatoes, peeled and diced
2 cloves garlic, minced
1 cup low-sodium chicken broth
1/4 cup unsweetened almond milk (or low-fat milk of your choice)
1 tablespoon unsalted butter (optional)
Chopped fresh parsley for garnish (optional)

Instructions:

Preheat the oven to 400°F (200°C).
Season the chicken breasts with salt and pepper. Heat the olive oil in an oven-safe skillet over medium-high heat. Add the chicken breasts and cook for about 3-4 minutes per side until browned. Transfer the skillet to the preheated oven and bake for another 10-15 minutes, or until the chicken is cooked through and reaches an internal temperature of 165°F (74°C). Remove the skillet from the oven and set aside.
In a large pot, bring water to a boil. Add the diced celery root and potatoes to the boiling water and cook for about 10-15 minutes, or until they are tender.
Drain the cooked celery root and potatoes, then transfer them to a food processor or blender. Add the minced garlic, low-sodium chicken broth, unsweetened almond milk, and a pinch of salt and pepper. Blend until smooth and creamy. If desired, you can add butter for added richness.
Transfer the celery root puree to a serving dish.
Place a cooked chicken breast on top of a portion of celery root puree.
Garnish with chopped fresh parsley if desired.
Serve the chicken with celery root puree while hot.

Ginger Salmon with Brown Rice

Ingredients:

4 salmon fillets (about 4-6 ounces each)
2 tablespoons low-sodium soy sauce
1 tablespoon fresh ginger, grated
2 cloves garlic, minced
1 tablespoon honey or a sugar substitute of your choice
1 tablespoon sesame oil
2 cups cooked brown rice
Steamed broccoli or your choice of vegetables, for serving
Optional garnish: sliced green onions, sesame seeds

Instructions:

Preheat the oven to 400°F (200°C).
In a small bowl, whisk together the low-sodium soy sauce, grated ginger, minced garlic, honey (or sugar substitute), and sesame oil to make the marinade.
Place the salmon fillets in a shallow dish and pour the marinade over them. Make sure the fillets are well coated on all sides. Let the salmon marinate for about 15-20 minutes.
Line a baking sheet with parchment paper or lightly grease it with cooking spray. Place the marinated salmon fillets on the baking sheet, leaving some space between each fillet.
Bake the salmon in the preheated oven for about 12-15 minutes, or until it flakes easily with a fork and reaches an internal temperature of 145°F (63°C).
While the salmon is baking, cook the brown rice according to package instructions.
Serve the cooked ginger salmon on a bed of cooked brown rice. Add steamed broccoli or your choice of vegetables on the side.
Garnish with sliced green onions and sesame seeds if desired.
Enjoy this flavorful Ginger Salmon with Brown Rice! Remember to adjust the portion sizes and ingredients based on your specific dietary needs and consult with a healthcare professional or registered dietitian for personalized advice.

Curry Turkey Stir-Fry

Ingredients:

1 pound turkey breast, thinly sliced
1 tablespoon olive oil
1 small onion, sliced
2 cloves garlic, minced
1 red bell pepper, sliced
1 green bell pepper, sliced
1 cup broccoli florets
2 carrots, sliced
1 tablespoon curry powder
1/2 teaspoon ground turmeric
1/2 teaspoon ground cumin
1/4 teaspoon cayenne pepper (optional, adjust to taste)
1 cup low-sodium chicken broth
1 tablespoon low-sodium soy sauce
Salt and pepper to taste
Chopped fresh cilantro for garnish (optional)
Cooked brown rice or quinoa, for serving

Instructions:

In a large skillet or wok, heat the olive oil over medium-high heat. Add the sliced turkey breast and cook for about 4-5 minutes, or until the turkey is browned and cooked through. Remove the turkey from the skillet and set it aside.
In the same skillet, add the sliced onion and minced garlic. Sauté for about 2-3 minutes, or until the onion is softened and fragrant.
Add the sliced red bell pepper, green bell pepper, broccoli florets, and sliced carrots to the skillet. Cook for another 4-5 minutes, or until the vegetables are tender-crisp.
In a small bowl, whisk together the curry powder, ground turmeric, ground cumin, cayenne pepper (if using), low-sodium chicken broth, and low-sodium soy sauce.
Pour the curry mixture into the skillet with the cooked vegetables. Stir well to combine.
Return the cooked turkey to the skillet and toss everything together. Cook for an additional 2-3 minutes to heat the turkey through and allow the flavors to meld together.
Season with salt and pepper to taste.
Serve the curry turkey stir-fry over cooked brown rice or quinoa. Garnish with chopped fresh cilantro if desired.

Pork with Sweet Potatoes

Ingredients:

1 pound pork tenderloin, cut into 1-inch cubes
2 tablespoons olive oil
1 small onion, diced
2 cloves garlic, minced
2 medium sweet potatoes, peeled and cubed
1 teaspoon ground cumin
1 teaspoon paprika
1/2 teaspoon ground cinnamon
1/4 teaspoon cayenne pepper (optional, adjust to taste)
Salt and pepper to taste
1 cup low-sodium chicken broth
Chopped fresh parsley for garnish (optional)

Instructions:

Heat the olive oil in a large skillet or Dutch oven over medium-high heat. Add the diced onion and minced garlic. Sauté for about 2-3 minutes until the onion is softened and fragrant.
Add the cubed pork tenderloin to the skillet and cook until browned on all sides, about 4-5 minutes. Remove the pork from the skillet and set it aside.
In the same skillet, add the cubed sweet potatoes. Sauté for about 5 minutes, or until the sweet potatoes start to soften slightly.
Add the ground cumin, paprika, ground cinnamon, cayenne pepper (if using), salt, and pepper to the skillet. Stir well to coat the sweet potatoes and onions with the spices.
Return the browned pork cubes to the skillet with the sweet potatoes. Stir everything together to combine.
Pour the low-sodium chicken broth into the skillet. Bring it to a simmer, then reduce the heat to low. Cover the skillet and let the pork and sweet potatoes simmer for about 15-20 minutes, or until the pork is cooked through and the sweet potatoes are tender.
Check the seasoning and adjust with salt and pepper if needed.
Serve the pork with sweet potatoes hot, garnished with chopped fresh parsley if desired.
Enjoy this delicious Pork with Sweet Potatoes! Remember to adjust the portion sizes and ingredients based on your specific dietary needs and consult with a healthcare professional or registered dietitian for personalized advice.

Grecian Pasta & Chicken Skillet

Ingredients:

8 ounces whole wheat pasta
1 tablespoon olive oil
1 pound boneless, skinless chicken breasts, cut into bite-sized pieces
1 medium onion, diced
2 cloves garlic, minced
1 red bell pepper, sliced
1 green bell pepper, sliced
1 can (14 ounces) diced tomatoes, no added sugar
1 tablespoon dried oregano
1 tablespoon dried basil
1/2 teaspoon salt (or to taste)
1/4 teaspoon black pepper (or to taste)
1/4 cup crumbled feta cheese
Fresh parsley for garnish (optional)

Instructions:

Cook the whole wheat pasta according to the package instructions. Drain and set aside.
Heat olive oil in a large skillet over medium-high heat. Add the chicken pieces and cook until they are no longer pink in the center. Remove the chicken from the skillet and set aside.
In the same skillet, add the diced onion and minced garlic. Sauté until the onion becomes translucent and fragrant.
Add the sliced red and green bell peppers to the skillet and cook until they are tender-crisp.
Stir in the diced tomatoes, dried oregano, dried basil, salt, and black pepper. Cook for a few minutes to allow the flavors to meld together.
Return the cooked chicken to the skillet and mix well with the sauce.
Add the cooked whole wheat pasta to the skillet and toss until everything is well combined and heated through.
Serve the Grecian pasta and chicken skillet in individual bowls. Sprinkle each serving with crumbled feta cheese and garnish with fresh parsley, if desired.
Enjoy your delicious and diabetic-friendly Grecian Pasta & Chicken Skillet!

Chicken-Stuffed Cubanelle Peppers

Ingredients:

4 Cubanelle peppers (also known as Italian frying peppers)
1 tablespoon olive oil
1 pound ground chicken (you can also use ground turkey)
1 small onion, diced
2 cloves garlic, minced
1/2 teaspoon dried oregano
1/2 teaspoon dried basil
1/4 teaspoon red pepper flakes (optional, adjust to taste)
1/2 teaspoon salt (or to taste)
1/4 teaspoon black pepper (or to taste)
1 cup low-sodium chicken broth
1/4 cup grated Parmesan cheese
Chopped fresh parsley for garnish (optional)

Instructions:

Preheat your oven to 375°F (190°C). Prepare a baking dish by lightly greasing it with cooking spray.
Cut the tops off the Cubanelle peppers and remove the seeds and membranes from the inside. Rinse the peppers under cold water and pat them dry.
Heat olive oil in a skillet over medium heat. Add the ground chicken and cook until it is no longer pink, breaking it up into small crumbles with a spoon or spatula.
Add the diced onion, minced garlic, dried oregano, dried basil, red pepper flakes (if using), salt, and black pepper to the skillet. Sauté until the onion becomes translucent and the spices are fragrant.
Pour in the chicken broth and bring it to a simmer. Cook for a few minutes until the broth has reduced slightly.
Remove the skillet from the heat and stir in the grated Parmesan cheese. Mix until the cheese is melted and well combined with the chicken mixture.
Spoon the chicken mixture into the prepared Cubanelle peppers, filling them generously.
Place the stuffed peppers in the baking dish and cover it with foil. Bake in the preheated oven for about 25-30 minutes or until the peppers are tender.
Once cooked, remove the foil and optionally sprinkle some additional grated Parmesan cheese on top of each pepper. Return the baking dish to the oven for a few more minutes until the cheese is melted and slightly golden.
Remove from the oven and let the stuffed peppers cool for a few minutes. Garnish with chopped fresh parsley, if desired, and serve.
Enjoy your delicious and diabetic-friendly Chicken-Stuffed Cubanelle Peppers!

Mediterranean Turkey Skillet

Ingredients:

1 pound ground turkey
1 tablespoon olive oil
1 small onion, diced
2 cloves garlic, minced
1 red bell pepper, diced
1 yellow bell pepper, diced
1 can (14 ounces) diced tomatoes, no added sugar
1/2 cup pitted Kalamata olives, sliced
1 tablespoon dried oregano
1 tablespoon dried basil
1/2 teaspoon dried thyme
1/2 teaspoon salt (or to taste)
1/4 teaspoon black pepper (or to taste)
1/4 cup crumbled feta cheese
Fresh parsley for garnish (optional)

Instructions:

Heat olive oil in a large skillet over medium-high heat. Add the ground turkey and cook until it is no longer pink, breaking it up into small crumbles with a spoon or spatula.
Add the diced onion and minced garlic to the skillet. Sauté until the onion becomes translucent and the garlic is fragrant.
Add the diced red and yellow bell peppers to the skillet and cook until they are tender-crisp.
Stir in the diced tomatoes (with their juice), sliced Kalamata olives, dried oregano, dried basil, dried thyme, salt, and black pepper. Cook for a few minutes to allow the flavors to meld together.
Reduce the heat to low and let the skillet simmer for about 10-15 minutes, allowing the flavors to further develop and the sauce to thicken slightly.
Sprinkle the crumbled feta cheese over the top of the turkey mixture. Cover the skillet and let it cook for a few more minutes until the cheese melts.
Remove from heat and let the skillet cool for a few minutes. Garnish with fresh parsley, if desired, and serve.
This Mediterranean Turkey Skillet is delicious on its own, but you can also serve it over cooked quinoa, whole wheat couscous, or with a side of steamed vegetables for a complete meal.

Enjoy your flavorful and diabetic-friendly Mediterranean Turkey Skillet!

Lemon-Basil Chicken Rotini

Ingredients:

8 ounces whole wheat rotini pasta
1 tablespoon olive oil
1 pound boneless, skinless chicken breasts, cut into bite-sized pieces
2 cloves garlic, minced
Zest of 1 lemon
Juice of 1 lemon
1 cup low-sodium chicken broth
1 teaspoon dried basil
1/2 teaspoon salt (or to taste)
1/4 teaspoon black pepper (or to taste)
2 cups baby spinach leaves
1/4 cup grated Parmesan cheese
Fresh basil leaves for garnish (optional)

Instructions:

Cook the whole wheat rotini pasta according to the package instructions. Drain and set aside.
Heat olive oil in a large skillet over medium-high heat. Add the chicken pieces and cook until they are no longer pink in the center. Remove the chicken from the skillet and set aside.
In the same skillet, add the minced garlic and lemon zest. Sauté for a minute until fragrant.
Pour in the lemon juice and chicken broth, scraping the bottom of the skillet to release any browned bits. Bring the mixture to a simmer.
Stir in the dried basil, salt, and black pepper. Let the sauce simmer for a few minutes to allow the flavors to meld together.
Add the cooked rotini pasta to the skillet and toss to coat it evenly with the lemon-basil sauce.
Add the cooked chicken and baby spinach leaves to the skillet. Stir everything together and cook for a couple more minutes until the spinach wilts.
Remove from heat and sprinkle the grated Parmesan cheese over the pasta. Toss again to combine and allow the cheese to melt slightly.
Garnish with fresh basil leaves, if desired, and serve.
This Lemon-Basil Chicken Rotini is a light and flavorful dish that's perfect for a diabetic-friendly meal. You can also add some cherry tomatoes or roasted vegetables for extra color and nutrients.

Enjoy your delicious and diabetic-friendly Lemon-Basil Chicken Rotini!

Chicken Butternut Chili

Ingredients:

1 tablespoon olive oil
1 pound boneless, skinless chicken breasts, cut into bite-sized pieces
1 small onion, diced
2 cloves garlic, minced
1 small butternut squash, peeled, seeded, and diced into small cubes
1 red bell pepper, diced
1 can (14 ounces) diced tomatoes, no added sugar
1 can (15 ounces) kidney beans, drained and rinsed
1 cup low-sodium chicken broth
1 tablespoon chili powder
1 teaspoon ground cumin
1/2 teaspoon dried oregano
1/2 teaspoon salt (or to taste)
1/4 teaspoon black pepper (or to taste)
Chopped fresh cilantro for garnish (optional)

Instructions:

Heat olive oil in a large pot or Dutch oven over medium-high heat. Add the chicken pieces and cook until they are no longer pink in the center. Remove the chicken from the pot and set aside.
In the same pot, add the diced onion and minced garlic. Sauté until the onion becomes translucent and fragrant.
Add the diced butternut squash and red bell pepper to the pot. Cook for a few minutes until the vegetables begin to soften.
Stir in the diced tomatoes (with their juice), kidney beans, chicken broth, chili powder, ground cumin, dried oregano, salt, and black pepper. Mix well to combine.
Bring the mixture to a boil, then reduce the heat to low. Cover the pot and let the chili simmer for about 20-25 minutes, or until the butternut squash is tender.
Return the cooked chicken to the pot and simmer for an additional 5 minutes to heat through.
Remove from heat and let the chili cool for a few minutes. Taste and adjust the seasoning if needed.
Serve the Chicken Butternut Chili in bowls, garnished with chopped fresh cilantro, if desired.
This Chicken Butternut Chili is a hearty and flavorful dish that's perfect for colder days. It's low in added sugars and high in protein and fiber, making it suitable for a diabetic-friendly diet.

Enjoy your delicious and diabetic-friendly Chicken Butternut Chili!

Italian Sausage Orzo

Ingredients:

8 ounces whole wheat orzo pasta
1 tablespoon olive oil
4 links (about 12 ounces) Italian turkey sausage, casings removed
1 small onion, diced
2 cloves garlic, minced
1 red bell pepper, diced
1 yellow bell pepper, diced
1 can (14 ounces) diced tomatoes, no added sugar
1/2 teaspoon dried basil
1/2 teaspoon dried oregano
1/2 teaspoon dried thyme
1/2 teaspoon salt (or to taste)
1/4 teaspoon black pepper (or to taste)
2 cups baby spinach leaves
Grated Parmesan cheese for serving (optional)
Fresh basil leaves for garnish (optional)

Instructions:

Cook the whole wheat orzo pasta according to the package instructions. Drain and set aside.
Heat olive oil in a large skillet over medium-high heat. Add the Italian turkey sausage and cook, breaking it up into crumbles with a spoon or spatula, until it is browned and cooked through. Remove the sausage from the skillet and set aside.
In the same skillet, add the diced onion and minced garlic. Sauté until the onion becomes translucent and the garlic is fragrant.
Add the diced red and yellow bell peppers to the skillet and cook until they are tender-crisp.
Stir in the diced tomatoes (with their juice), dried basil, dried oregano, dried thyme, salt, and black pepper. Cook for a few minutes to allow the flavors to meld together.
Add the cooked orzo pasta and cooked Italian turkey sausage to the skillet. Mix everything together until well combined.
Add the baby spinach leaves to the skillet and toss until they wilt and become incorporated into the dish.
Remove from heat and let the Italian Sausage Orzo cool for a few minutes. Serve in bowls, optionally topped with grated Parmesan cheese and garnished with fresh basil leaves.
This Italian Sausage Orzo is packed with flavor and protein. The whole wheat orzo provides a good source of fiber, making it a balanced and satisfying dish for a diabetic-friendly meal.

Enjoy your delicious and diabetic-friendly Italian Sausage Orzo!

Bow Ties with Sausage & Asparagus

Ingredients:

8 ounces whole wheat bow tie pasta
1 tablespoon olive oil
4 links (about 12 ounces) Italian turkey sausage, casings removed
1 bunch asparagus, trimmed and cut into 1-inch pieces
1 small onion, diced
2 cloves garlic, minced
1/2 cup low-sodium chicken broth
1/2 teaspoon dried basil
1/2 teaspoon dried oregano
1/2 teaspoon dried thyme
1/2 teaspoon salt (or to taste)
1/4 teaspoon black pepper (or to taste)
Grated Parmesan cheese for serving (optional)
Fresh parsley for garnish (optional)

Instructions:

Cook the whole wheat bow tie pasta according to the package instructions. Drain and set aside.
Heat olive oil in a large skillet over medium-high heat. Add the Italian turkey sausage and cook, breaking it up into crumbles with a spoon or spatula, until it is browned and cooked through. Remove the sausage from the skillet and set aside.
In the same skillet, add the diced onion and minced garlic. Sauté until the onion becomes translucent and the garlic is fragrant.
Add the asparagus pieces to the skillet and cook for a few minutes until they are tender-crisp.
Stir in the cooked Italian turkey sausage, dried basil, dried oregano, dried thyme, salt, and black pepper. Mix well to combine.
Pour the chicken broth into the skillet and bring it to a simmer. Cook for a few minutes to allow the flavors to meld together.
Add the cooked bow tie pasta to the skillet and toss until everything is well combined and heated through.
Remove from heat and let the Bow Ties with Sausage & Asparagus cool for a few minutes. Serve in bowls, optionally topped with grated Parmesan cheese and garnished with fresh parsley.
This Bow Ties with Sausage & Asparagus dish is a flavorful and well-balanced option for a diabetic-friendly meal. The whole wheat pasta adds fiber, and the asparagus provides vitamins and minerals.

Enjoy your delicious and diabetic-friendly Bow Ties with Sausage & Asparagus!

Turkey Cabbage Stew

Ingredients:

1 lb ground turkey
1 small onion, diced
2 cloves garlic, minced
4 cups cabbage, thinly sliced
2 carrots, peeled and sliced
2 celery stalks, sliced
1 can (14.5 oz) diced tomatoes (no added sugar)
4 cups low-sodium chicken broth
1 teaspoon dried thyme
1 bay leaf
Salt and pepper to taste
1 tablespoon olive oil

Instructions:

Heat olive oil in a large pot over medium heat. Add the ground turkey and cook until browned, breaking it up into small pieces with a spoon.

Add the diced onion and minced garlic to the pot. Cook for a few minutes until the onion is translucent and fragrant.

Add the sliced cabbage, carrots, and celery to the pot. Stir everything together and cook for about 5 minutes until the vegetables start to soften.

Pour in the diced tomatoes with their juice, chicken broth, dried thyme, and bay leaf. Season with salt and pepper to taste. Stir well to combine all the ingredients.

Bring the stew to a boil, then reduce the heat to low. Cover the pot and let it simmer for about 30-40 minutes, until the vegetables are tender and the flavors have melded together.

Remove the bay leaf before serving. Taste and adjust the seasoning if needed.

Ladle the Turkey Cabbage Stew into bowls and serve hot.

This recipe is packed with lean protein from the ground turkey and plenty of vegetables, making it a nutritious and diabetes-friendly option. Remember to consult with a healthcare professional or a registered dietitian for personalized advice regarding your specific dietary needs. Enjoy your stew!

Chinese Chicken Spaghetti

Ingredients:

8 oz whole wheat spaghetti
2 boneless, skinless chicken breasts, thinly sliced
2 tablespoons low-sodium soy sauce
1 tablespoon hoisin sauce
1 tablespoon sesame oil
1 tablespoon canola oil
1 cup broccoli florets
1 cup sliced bell peppers (any color)
1 cup sliced carrots
2 cloves garlic, minced
1 teaspoon grated ginger
2 green onions, sliced (white and green parts separated)
Salt and pepper to taste
Optional garnish: sesame seeds and chopped cilantro

Instructions:

Cook the whole wheat spaghetti according to the package instructions. Drain and set aside.
In a bowl, combine the sliced chicken breasts with the soy sauce and hoisin sauce. Allow the chicken to marinate for about 15 minutes.
Heat the canola oil in a large skillet or wok over medium-high heat. Add the marinated chicken slices and stir-fry until they are cooked through, about 5-6 minutes. Remove the cooked chicken from the skillet and set aside.
In the same skillet, add the sesame oil and heat over medium-high heat. Add the broccoli, bell peppers, carrots, garlic, ginger, and the white parts of the green onions. Stir-fry for about 3-4 minutes until the vegetables are crisp-tender.
Return the cooked chicken to the skillet with the vegetables. Add the cooked spaghetti and toss everything together. Stir-fry for another 2-3 minutes to heat through and allow the flavors to meld.
Season with salt and pepper to taste. Garnish with the green parts of the sliced green onions, sesame seeds, and chopped cilantro if desired.
Serve the Chinese Chicken Spaghetti hot.
This recipe combines the flavors of Chinese cuisine with spaghetti for a unique and delicious dish. Whole wheat spaghetti adds more fiber and nutrients compared to traditional white spaghetti. Remember to adjust portion sizes according to your specific dietary needs and consult with a healthcare professional or a registered dietitian for personalized advice. Enjoy your meal!

Shrimp & Corn Stir-Fry

Ingredients:

1 lb shrimp, peeled and deveined
2 cups fresh or frozen corn kernels
1 red bell pepper, sliced
1 small onion, sliced
2 cloves garlic, minced
1 tablespoon low-sodium soy sauce
1 tablespoon rice vinegar
1 teaspoon honey or a sugar substitute
1 teaspoon cornstarch (optional, for thickening)
1 tablespoon canola oil
Salt and pepper to taste
Optional garnish: sliced green onions and sesame seeds

Instructions:

In a small bowl, whisk together the soy sauce, rice vinegar, honey (or sugar substitute), and cornstarch (if using). Set aside.
Heat the canola oil in a large skillet or wok over medium-high heat.
Add the sliced onion and minced garlic to the skillet. Stir-fry for about 2-3 minutes until the onion starts to soften and become translucent.
Add the shrimp to the skillet and cook for about 3-4 minutes until they turn pink and opaque. Remove the cooked shrimp from the skillet and set aside.
In the same skillet, add the sliced bell pepper and corn kernels. Stir-fry for about 3-4 minutes until the vegetables are tender-crisp.
Return the cooked shrimp to the skillet with the vegetables. Pour the soy sauce mixture over everything and stir well to coat. Cook for another 1-2 minutes until the sauce thickens slightly.
Season with salt and pepper to taste. Garnish with sliced green onions and sesame seeds if desired.
Serve the Shrimp & Corn Stir-Fry hot.
This recipe is low in added sugars and contains lean protein from the shrimp and plenty of vegetables. It's important to adjust portion sizes according to your specific dietary needs and consult with a healthcare professional or a registered dietitian for personalized advice. Enjoy your stir-fry!

Sausage-Topped White Pizza

Ingredients:

1 whole wheat pizza crust (store-bought or homemade)
2 tablespoons olive oil
2 cloves garlic, minced
1 cup part-skim ricotta cheese
1 cup shredded mozzarella cheese (part-skim)
4 ounces turkey or chicken sausage, sliced
1 cup sliced mushrooms
1 cup fresh spinach leaves
1 teaspoon dried oregano
Salt and pepper to taste
Optional garnish: fresh basil leaves

Instructions:

Preheat your oven to the temperature recommended for the pizza crust.
In a small bowl, mix together the olive oil and minced garlic. Set aside.
Roll out the whole wheat pizza crust on a lightly floured surface or according to the package instructions.
Transfer the rolled-out pizza crust to a pizza stone or baking sheet.
Brush the olive oil and garlic mixture evenly over the surface of the pizza crust, leaving a small border around the edges.
Spread the ricotta cheese evenly over the crust, followed by the shredded mozzarella cheese.
Evenly distribute the sliced sausage, mushrooms, and spinach leaves over the cheese.
Sprinkle the dried oregano, salt, and pepper over the toppings.
Place the pizza in the preheated oven and bake according to the instructions for the pizza crust, or until the crust is golden and the cheese is melted and bubbly.
Remove the pizza from the oven and let it cool for a few minutes. Garnish with fresh basil leaves if desired.
Slice the pizza into wedges and serve.
This recipe uses whole wheat pizza crust and lean protein from turkey or chicken sausage to make it more diabetes-friendly. The use of part-skim cheeses helps reduce the overall fat content. Remember to adjust portion sizes according to your specific dietary needs and consult with a healthcare professional or a registered dietitian for personalized advice. Enjoy your pizza!

Lemon Salmon with Basil

Ingredients:

2 salmon fillets (4-6 ounces each)
2 tablespoons fresh lemon juice
Zest of 1 lemon
2 tablespoons fresh basil, chopped
1 tablespoon olive oil
2 cloves garlic, minced
Salt and pepper to taste
Lemon slices for garnish

Instructions:

Preheat your oven to 400°F (200°C). Line a baking sheet with parchment paper or foil.
In a small bowl, combine the fresh lemon juice, lemon zest, chopped basil, olive oil, minced garlic, salt, and pepper. Mix well to make a marinade.
Place the salmon fillets on the prepared baking sheet. Pour the marinade over the salmon, ensuring it is evenly coated.
Let the salmon marinate for about 15-20 minutes to allow the flavors to meld.
After marinating, place the baking sheet with the salmon in the preheated oven. Bake for approximately 12-15 minutes, or until the salmon is cooked through and flakes easily with a fork.
Once cooked, remove the salmon from the oven and let it rest for a few minutes.
Serve the Lemon Salmon with Basil hot, garnished with lemon slices.
This recipe uses fresh lemon juice and zest to add bright flavors to the salmon, while basil adds a refreshing herbal note. Remember to adjust portion sizes according to your specific dietary needs and consult with a healthcare professional or a registered dietitian for personalized advice. Pair the salmon with a side of steamed vegetables or a salad for a complete and balanced meal. Enjoy!

Chicken & Vegetable Kabobs

Ingredients:

1 lb boneless, skinless chicken breast, cut into 1-inch cubes
1 red bell pepper, cut into 1-inch pieces
1 green bell pepper, cut into 1-inch pieces
1 zucchini, sliced into rounds
1 red onion, cut into wedges
8-10 cherry tomatoes
2 tablespoons olive oil
2 cloves garlic, minced
1 teaspoon dried oregano
1 teaspoon dried basil
Salt and pepper to taste
Wooden or metal skewers

Instructions:

If using wooden skewers, soak them in water for about 20 minutes to prevent burning during grilling.
In a bowl, combine the olive oil, minced garlic, dried oregano, dried basil, salt, and pepper. Mix well to create a marinade.
Place the chicken cubes in a separate bowl and pour half of the marinade over the chicken. Toss to coat the chicken evenly. Let it marinate for about 15-20 minutes.
Preheat your grill or grill pan over medium-high heat.
Thread the marinated chicken, bell peppers, zucchini, red onion, and cherry tomatoes onto the skewers, alternating between ingredients.
Brush the remaining marinade onto the skewered chicken and vegetables.
Place the skewers on the preheated grill or grill pan. Cook for about 10-12 minutes, turning occasionally, until the chicken is cooked through and the vegetables are slightly charred.
Remove the kabobs from the grill and let them rest for a few minutes before serving.
Serve the Chicken & Vegetable Kabobs hot as a delicious and colorful meal.
This recipe provides lean protein from chicken breast and a variety of vegetables for added nutrients and fiber.
Remember to adjust portion sizes according to your specific dietary needs and consult with a healthcare professional or a registered dietitian for personalized advice. Enjoy your kabobs!

Chicken Thighs with Shallots & Spinach

Ingredients:

4 bone-in, skinless chicken thighs
Salt and pepper to taste
1 tablespoon olive oil
4 shallots, thinly sliced
2 cloves garlic, minced
1 cup low-sodium chicken broth
1 tablespoon Dijon mustard
2 cups fresh spinach leaves
1 tablespoon fresh lemon juice
Optional garnish: chopped parsley

Instructions:

Season the chicken thighs with salt and pepper on both sides.
Heat olive oil in a large skillet over medium-high heat. Add the chicken thighs to the skillet and cook for about 6-8 minutes per side, or until they are browned and cooked through. Remove the chicken thighs from the skillet and set aside.
In the same skillet, add the sliced shallots and minced garlic. Sauté for about 2-3 minutes until the shallots start to soften and become translucent.
Pour the chicken broth into the skillet and bring it to a simmer. Stir in the Dijon mustard and continue to simmer for about 3-4 minutes to allow the flavors to meld together.
Add the fresh spinach leaves to the skillet and cook for another 1-2 minutes until they wilt.
Return the chicken thighs to the skillet, nestling them into the shallot and spinach mixture. Cook for an additional 2-3 minutes to heat the chicken through.
Drizzle the fresh lemon juice over the chicken and vegetables. Stir gently to coat everything evenly.
Remove the skillet from the heat. Garnish with chopped parsley if desired.
Serve the Chicken Thighs with Shallots & Spinach hot as a flavorful and satisfying meal.
This recipe uses bone-in, skinless chicken thighs for added flavor and tenderness. The combination of shallots, garlic, and Dijon mustard adds depth to the dish, while the spinach provides added nutrients. Remember to adjust portion sizes according to your specific dietary needs and consult with a healthcare professional or a registered dietitian for personalized advice. Enjoy your meal!

Beef & Spinach Lo Mein

Ingredients:

8 oz whole wheat or brown rice spaghetti noodles
8 oz lean beef, thinly sliced (such as sirloin or flank steak)
2 tablespoons low-sodium soy sauce
1 tablespoon hoisin sauce
1 tablespoon oyster sauce (optional)
1 tablespoon sesame oil
1 tablespoon canola oil
2 cloves garlic, minced
1 teaspoon grated ginger
2 cups fresh spinach leaves
1 cup sliced mushrooms
1 cup sliced bell peppers (any color)
1 cup shredded carrots
2 green onions, sliced (white and green parts separated)
Salt and pepper to taste

Instructions:

Cook the spaghetti noodles according to the package instructions. Drain and set aside.
In a bowl, combine the sliced beef with the soy sauce, hoisin sauce, and oyster sauce (if using). Allow the beef to marinate for about 15 minutes.
Heat the canola oil and sesame oil in a large skillet or wok over medium-high heat.
Add the minced garlic and grated ginger to the skillet. Stir-fry for about 1-2 minutes until fragrant.
Add the marinated beef slices to the skillet and cook for about 3-4 minutes until they are browned and cooked through. Remove the cooked beef from the skillet and set aside.
In the same skillet, add the sliced mushrooms, bell peppers, shredded carrots, and white parts of the sliced green onions. Stir-fry for about 3-4 minutes until the vegetables are tender-crisp.
Add the fresh spinach leaves to the skillet and cook for another 1-2 minutes until they wilt.
Return the cooked beef to the skillet with the vegetables. Add the cooked spaghetti noodles to the skillet as well.
Pour the remaining marinade sauce over the beef, vegetables, and noodles. Stir everything together to combine and heat through.
Season with salt and pepper to taste. Garnish with the green parts of the sliced green onions.
Serve the Beef & Spinach Lo Mein hot.
This recipe uses whole wheat or brown rice noodles for added fiber and nutrients. Lean beef and plenty of vegetables provide a balanced and satisfying meal. Remember to adjust portion sizes according to your specific dietary needs and consult with a healthcare professional or a registered dietitian for personalized advice. Enjoy your Lo Mein!

Mediterranean Pork and Orzo

Ingredients:

1 lb pork tenderloin, cut into 1-inch cubes
Salt and pepper to taste
2 tablespoons olive oil, divided
1 onion, finely chopped
3 cloves garlic, minced
1 red bell pepper, diced
1 zucchini, diced
1 cup cherry tomatoes, halved
1 cup cooked orzo pasta
1 tablespoon lemon juice
1 teaspoon dried oregano
1 teaspoon dried basil
½ teaspoon dried thyme
½ cup crumbled feta cheese
Fresh parsley, chopped (for garnish)

Instructions:

Season the pork tenderloin cubes with salt and pepper.
Heat 1 tablespoon of olive oil in a large skillet over medium-high heat. Add the pork cubes and cook for about 4-5 minutes, or until browned on all sides. Remove the pork from the skillet and set aside.
In the same skillet, add the remaining 1 tablespoon of olive oil. Add the chopped onion and minced garlic, and sauté for 2-3 minutes until the onion becomes translucent.
Add the diced red bell pepper and zucchini to the skillet. Sauté for another 3-4 minutes until the vegetables are slightly softened.
Return the cooked pork cubes to the skillet with the vegetables. Stir in the halved cherry tomatoes, cooked orzo pasta, lemon juice, dried oregano, dried basil, and dried thyme. Cook for an additional 2-3 minutes to heat everything through.
Remove the skillet from the heat and sprinkle the crumbled feta cheese over the pork and orzo mixture. Toss gently to combine.
Garnish with fresh parsley.
Serve the Mediterranean Pork and Orzo hot as a flavorful and wholesome dish.
This recipe combines tender pork, Mediterranean vegetables, and orzo pasta for a satisfying meal. Adjust seasonings according to your taste preferences and dietary needs. Remember to consult with a healthcare professional or a registered dietitian for personalized advice. Enjoy your Mediterranean feast!

Green Pepper Steak

Ingredients:

1 lb beef sirloin or flank steak, thinly sliced
2 green bell peppers, sliced
1 onion, sliced
2 cloves garlic, minced
2 tablespoons low-sodium soy sauce
1 tablespoon oyster sauce
1 tablespoon cornstarch
1 teaspoon sugar or a sugar substitute
1/2 cup low-sodium beef broth
2 tablespoons vegetable oil
Salt and pepper to taste
Optional garnish: sliced green onions

Instructions:

In a small bowl, whisk together the soy sauce, oyster sauce, cornstarch, sugar, and beef broth. Set aside.
Heat the vegetable oil in a large skillet or wok over high heat.
Add the sliced beef to the skillet and cook for about 2-3 minutes until browned. Remove the beef from the skillet and set aside.
In the same skillet, add the sliced green bell peppers, onion, and minced garlic. Stir-fry for about 3-4 minutes until the vegetables are tender-crisp.
Return the cooked beef to the skillet with the vegetables.
Give the sauce mixture a quick stir and pour it over the beef and vegetables in the skillet.
Cook for another 1-2 minutes, stirring continuously, until the sauce thickens and coats the beef and vegetables evenly.
Season with salt and pepper to taste.
Remove the skillet from the heat.
Garnish with sliced green onions if desired.
Serve the Green Pepper Steak hot with steamed rice or cauliflower rice for a complete meal.
This recipe offers a flavorful combination of beef, green bell peppers, and a savory sauce. Adjust the seasoning and sugar levels according to your taste preferences and dietary needs. Remember to consult with a healthcare professional or a registered dietitian for personalized advice. Enjoy your Green Pepper Steak!

Skillet Sea Scallops

Ingredients:

1 pound sea scallops
2 tablespoons olive oil
Salt and pepper to taste
2 tablespoons butter
2 cloves garlic, minced
1/4 cup white wine or chicken broth
Juice of 1 lemon
2 tablespoons chopped fresh parsley

Instructions:

Start by patting the sea scallops dry with a paper towel to remove any excess moisture. This will help them sear properly.
Heat the olive oil in a large skillet over medium-high heat.
Season the scallops with salt and pepper on both sides.
Carefully add the scallops to the hot skillet, making sure they are not touching each other. Cook them in batches if necessary.
Let the scallops cook undisturbed for about 2-3 minutes or until a golden brown crust forms on the bottom. Avoid moving them around too much as this can prevent proper browning.
Flip the scallops using a pair of tongs and cook for an additional 2-3 minutes on the other side until they are opaque and cooked through. The cooking time may vary depending on the size of the scallops, so keep an eye on them to prevent overcooking.
Transfer the cooked scallops to a plate and cover them with foil to keep warm.
Reduce the heat to medium and add the butter to the skillet. Allow it to melt and then add the minced garlic. Sauté for about 1 minute until fragrant, being careful not to burn the garlic.
Pour in the white wine or chicken broth and lemon juice. Stir well, scraping any browned bits from the bottom of the skillet.
Let the sauce simmer for a couple of minutes until it slightly thickens.
Return the scallops to the skillet and toss them in the sauce to coat.
Sprinkle with chopped parsley and give it a final toss.
Remove from heat and serve the skillet sea scallops immediately as a main dish or with your favorite side dishes.
Enjoy your delicious Skillet Sea Scallops!

Chicken Sausages with Peppers

Ingredients:

4 chicken sausages
2 tablespoons olive oil
1 large onion, thinly sliced
2 bell peppers (any color), thinly sliced
3 cloves garlic, minced
1 teaspoon dried oregano
Salt and pepper to taste
1/4 cup chicken broth or water
Optional toppings: fresh parsley, grated Parmesan cheese

Instructions:

Heat 1 tablespoon of olive oil in a large skillet over medium heat.
Add the chicken sausages to the skillet and cook until browned on all sides. This will take about 8-10 minutes. Remove the sausages from the skillet and set them aside.
In the same skillet, add the remaining tablespoon of olive oil and heat it up.
Add the sliced onion and bell peppers to the skillet. Sauté them for about 5 minutes until they start to soften.
Stir in the minced garlic, dried oregano, salt, and pepper. Cook for an additional 2 minutes until the garlic becomes fragrant.
Pour in the chicken broth or water to deglaze the skillet, scraping any browned bits from the bottom.
Reduce the heat to low and return the chicken sausages to the skillet, nestling them among the peppers and onions.
Cover the skillet and let the sausages and peppers simmer for about 10-15 minutes until the sausages are fully cooked and the peppers are tender.
Remove the lid and give everything a stir to combine the flavors.
Taste and adjust the seasoning if needed.
Serve the chicken sausages and peppers hot, either on their own or as a sandwich filling.
If desired, garnish with fresh parsley and grated Parmesan cheese before serving.
Enjoy your Chicken Sausages with Peppers!

Crunchy Oven-Baked Tilapia

Ingredients:

4 tilapia fillets
1 cup breadcrumbs (plain or seasoned)
1/2 cup grated Parmesan cheese
1 teaspoon garlic powder
1/2 teaspoon paprika
Salt and pepper to taste
2 eggs, beaten
Cooking spray or olive oil

Instructions:

Preheat your oven to 425°F (220°C) and lightly grease a baking sheet with cooking spray or olive oil.
In a shallow bowl or dish, combine the breadcrumbs, grated Parmesan cheese, garlic powder, paprika, salt, and pepper. Mix well.
Dip each tilapia fillet into the beaten eggs, allowing any excess to drip off.
Press the dipped fillets into the breadcrumb mixture, coating both sides thoroughly. Press the mixture onto the fillets to ensure good coverage and adherence.
Place the coated tilapia fillets onto the prepared baking sheet in a single layer.
Lightly spray the tops of the fillets with cooking spray or drizzle with a little olive oil. This will help them become crispy and golden.
Bake the tilapia in the preheated oven for about 12-15 minutes, or until the fish is cooked through and the coating is crispy and golden brown.
Remove the baking sheet from the oven and let the tilapia rest for a couple of minutes.
Serve the Crunchy Oven-Baked Tilapia hot with your favorite side dishes or a squeeze of lemon for extra freshness.
Enjoy your delicious Crunchy Oven-Baked Tilapia!

Stir-Fry Rice Bowl

Ingredients:

2 cups cooked rice (white or brown)
1 tablespoon vegetable oil
2 cloves garlic, minced
1 small onion, diced
1 carrot, julienned
1 bell pepper, thinly sliced
1 cup broccoli florets
1 cup sliced mushrooms
1 cup protein of your choice (chicken, beef, shrimp, tofu), thinly sliced or cubed
3 tablespoons soy sauce
1 tablespoon oyster sauce (optional)
1 tablespoon hoisin sauce (optional)
1 teaspoon sesame oil
Salt and pepper to taste
Optional toppings: sliced green onions, sesame seeds

Instructions:

Heat the vegetable oil in a large skillet or wok over medium-high heat.
Add the minced garlic and diced onion to the skillet. Stir-fry for 1-2 minutes until fragrant and the onion begins to soften.
Add the julienned carrot, sliced bell pepper, broccoli florets, and sliced mushrooms to the skillet. Stir-fry for about 3-4 minutes until the vegetables are tender-crisp.
Push the vegetables to one side of the skillet and add the protein (chicken, beef, shrimp, tofu) to the empty space. Cook until the protein is fully cooked through.
In a small bowl, whisk together the soy sauce, oyster sauce, hoisin sauce (if using), and sesame oil.
Pour the sauce mixture over the cooked vegetables and protein in the skillet. Stir-fry everything together for an additional 1-2 minutes to coat everything evenly.
Add the cooked rice to the skillet and mix well with the vegetables and protein. Stir-fry for another 2-3 minutes until the rice is heated through and well combined with the other ingredients.
Taste and season with salt and pepper as needed.
Remove from heat and transfer the Stir-Fry Rice Bowl to serving bowls.
Garnish with sliced green onions and sesame seeds, if desired.
Serve the Stir-Fry Rice Bowl hot as a complete meal or with additional sides.
Enjoy your flavorful Stir-Fry Rice Bowl!

Curry Turkey Stir-Fry

Ingredients:

1 pound turkey breast, thinly sliced
2 tablespoons vegetable oil
1 onion, thinly sliced
2 cloves garlic, minced
1 red bell pepper, thinly sliced
1 yellow bell pepper, thinly sliced
1 zucchini, thinly sliced
1 tablespoon curry powder
1 teaspoon ground cumin
1 teaspoon ground coriander
1/2 teaspoon turmeric
1/2 teaspoon paprika
1 cup coconut milk
2 tablespoons soy sauce
Juice of 1 lime
Salt and pepper to taste
Fresh cilantro for garnish

Instructions:

Heat the vegetable oil in a large skillet or wok over medium-high heat.
Add the thinly sliced turkey breast to the skillet and stir-fry until it's cooked through and lightly browned. Remove the turkey from the skillet and set it aside.
In the same skillet, add the sliced onion and minced garlic. Sauté for about 2-3 minutes until the onion becomes translucent and the garlic is fragrant.
Add the sliced red and yellow bell peppers, along with the zucchini, to the skillet. Stir-fry for another 3-4 minutes until the vegetables start to soften.
In a small bowl, combine the curry powder, ground cumin, ground coriander, turmeric, and paprika. Mix well to create a spice blend.
Sprinkle the spice blend over the vegetables in the skillet and stir-fry for about 1 minute until the spices are aromatic.
Pour in the coconut milk, soy sauce, and lime juice. Stir well to combine all the ingredients and bring the mixture to a simmer.
Return the cooked turkey to the skillet and stir-fry everything together for an additional 2-3 minutes until the flavors meld and the turkey is heated through.
Taste the stir-fry and season with salt and pepper according to your preference.
Remove from heat and transfer the Curry Turkey Stir-Fry to serving plates.
Garnish with fresh cilantro leaves.
Serve the Curry Turkey Stir-Fry hot over rice or noodles.
Enjoy your flavorful Curry Turkey Stir-Fry!

Mediterranean Tilapia

Ingredients:

4 tilapia fillets
2 tablespoons olive oil
2 cloves garlic, minced
1 teaspoon dried oregano
1 teaspoon dried basil
1/2 teaspoon dried thyme
Juice of 1 lemon
Salt and pepper to taste
1 cup cherry tomatoes, halved
1/4 cup pitted Kalamata olives, sliced
2 tablespoons capers
Fresh parsley for garnish

Instructions:

Preheat your oven to 400°F (200°C).
Place the tilapia fillets in a baking dish and drizzle them with olive oil.
Sprinkle minced garlic, dried oregano, dried basil, and dried thyme over the fillets.
Squeeze the juice of one lemon over the fillets and season with salt and pepper to taste.
Gently toss the cherry tomatoes, Kalamata olives, and capers together in a bowl.
Spoon the tomato, olive, and caper mixture evenly over the tilapia fillets.
Cover the baking dish with aluminum foil and bake in the preheated oven for about 15-20 minutes, or until the tilapia is cooked through and flakes easily with a fork.
Remove the foil and broil the dish for an additional 2-3 minutes to lightly brown the top.
Garnish with fresh parsley before serving.
Serve the Mediterranean Tilapia hot with a side of roasted vegetables, rice, or a salad.
Enjoy your flavorful Mediterranean Tilapia!

Rosemary Garlic Shrimp

Ingredients:

1 pound large shrimp, peeled and deveined
3 tablespoons olive oil
4 cloves garlic, minced
1 tablespoon fresh rosemary leaves, finely chopped
Juice of 1 lemon
Salt and pepper to taste
Optional: Red pepper flakes for added heat
Optional: Lemon wedges and fresh parsley for garnish

Instructions:

In a bowl, combine the olive oil, minced garlic, chopped rosemary, lemon juice, salt, pepper, and red pepper flakes (if using). Mix well to create a marinade.
Add the peeled and deveined shrimp to the bowl and toss them in the marinade until they are well coated.
Allow the shrimp to marinate for at least 15 minutes, or refrigerate for up to 1 hour for more flavor.
Heat a large skillet over medium-high heat.
Once the skillet is hot, add the marinated shrimp in a single layer, along with any remaining marinade.
Cook the shrimp for 2-3 minutes on one side until they start to turn pink and slightly curl.
Flip the shrimp and cook for another 2-3 minutes on the other side until they are opaque and cooked through. Be careful not to overcook them, as shrimp can become rubbery if cooked for too long.
Remove the skillet from heat and transfer the cooked shrimp to a serving platter.
Pour any remaining juices from the skillet over the shrimp for added flavor.
Garnish with lemon wedges and fresh parsley, if desired.
Serve the Rosemary Garlic Shrimp as an appetizer, main dish, or with a side of rice, pasta, or crusty bread.
Enjoy your flavorful Rosemary Garlic Shrimp!

Peppered Tuna Kabobs

Ingredients:

1 pound tuna steak, cut into 1-inch cubes
2 tablespoons olive oil
1 tablespoon lemon juice
2 cloves garlic, minced
1 teaspoon cracked black pepper
1/2 teaspoon salt
1 red bell pepper, cut into 1-inch pieces
1 yellow bell pepper, cut into 1-inch pieces
1 red onion, cut into 1-inch pieces
Optional: Cherry tomatoes, mushrooms, or other vegetables of your choice for kabob assembly
Skewers (if using wooden skewers, soak them in water for 30 minutes prior to grilling)

Instructions:

In a bowl, whisk together the olive oil, lemon juice, minced garlic, cracked black pepper, and salt to create a marinade.
Place the tuna cubes in the marinade and toss to coat. Let the tuna marinate for at least 15 minutes, or refrigerate for up to 1 hour for more flavor.
Preheat your grill to medium-high heat.
Thread the marinated tuna cubes onto skewers, alternating with pieces of red bell pepper, yellow bell pepper, and red onion (and any other desired vegetables).
Place the assembled kabobs on the preheated grill and cook for about 3-4 minutes per side, or until the tuna is seared on the outside but still slightly pink in the center. Be careful not to overcook the tuna, as it can become dry.
Remove the kabobs from the grill and let them rest for a few minutes before serving.
Serve the Peppered Tuna Kabobs hot as a main dish or alongside a salad, rice, or grilled vegetables.
Enjoy the delicious and flavorful Peppered Tuna Kabobs!
Note: You can also cook the kabobs under a broiler if you don't have access to a grill. Simply place them on a baking sheet and broil for about 3-4 minutes per side, or until the tuna is cooked to your desired doneness.

I want to take a moment to express my heartfelt gratitude for your recent purchase of my recipe book. As a passionate food lover, nothing makes me happier than sharing my favorite recipes with others. Your decision to invest in my book not only supports my dream, but also shows your commitment to expanding your culinary horizons.

I sincerely hope that the recipes in the book will inspire you to try new things and add some excitement to your meals.

Thank you again for your support and for being a part of this journey with me. I hope my book will bring you many happy and delicious moments in the kitchen.

www.ingramcontent.com/pod-product-compliance
Lightning Source LLC
Chambersburg PA
CBHW081236080526
44587CB00022B/3962